THE STARRY SKY

The Stars

Patrick Moore

Illustrated by Paul Doherty

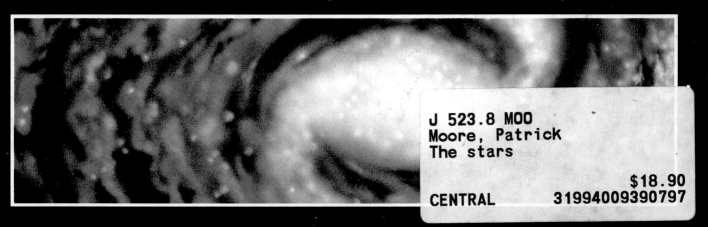

COPPER BEECH BOOKS

Produced by
Aladdin Books Limited
28 Percy Street
London W1P 9FF
Designed by David West Children's Book Design

First published 1994 in the United Kingdom by
Riverswift, Random House, London

First published 1995 in the United States by
Copper Beech Books
an imprint of
The Millbrook Press
2 Old New Milford Road
Brookfield, Connecticut 06804

3 5 4

Illustrations by Paul Doherty
Additional illustrations by Mike Lacey and Ian Thompson
Photocredits: Page 8: Science Photo Library

Library of Congress Cataloging-in-Publication Data
Moore, Patrick.
The stars / By Patrick Moore: illustrated by Paul Doherty.
p. cm. – (The starry sky)
Includes index
ISBN 1-56294-623-4 (lib. bdg.) 1-56294-641-2 (pbk.)
1. Stars–Juvenile literature. [1. Stars.] I. Doherty, Paul, ill. II. Title. III. Series.
QB801.7.M66 1995
523.8–dc20   94-43937
CIP   AC

*My grateful thanks are due to Paul Doherty for his splendid pictures, and to
Lynn Lockett for all her help and encouragement.*
                                                                P.M.

Contents

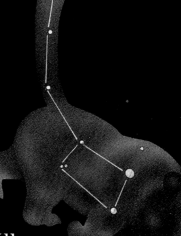

Looking at the
stars
When you look up into the sky at nighttime, you will see the stars. You cannot see the stars in the daytime because the sky is too bright, but they are always there. They seem to twinkle but this is only because the light from them has to come through the air above us. If the Earth had no air, the stars would not twinkle at all.

The sky is so full of stars that you may think

4

that you will never be able to tell one from another. But because the stars are so far away, the groups do not change, and this makes it easy to learn your way around. Soon you will recognize the different groups visible from your part of the Earth; you will be able to see the red and orange stars, the gas-clouds and much more. If you take a star-map and go out at night, you will quickly find that you are making friends with all the stars.

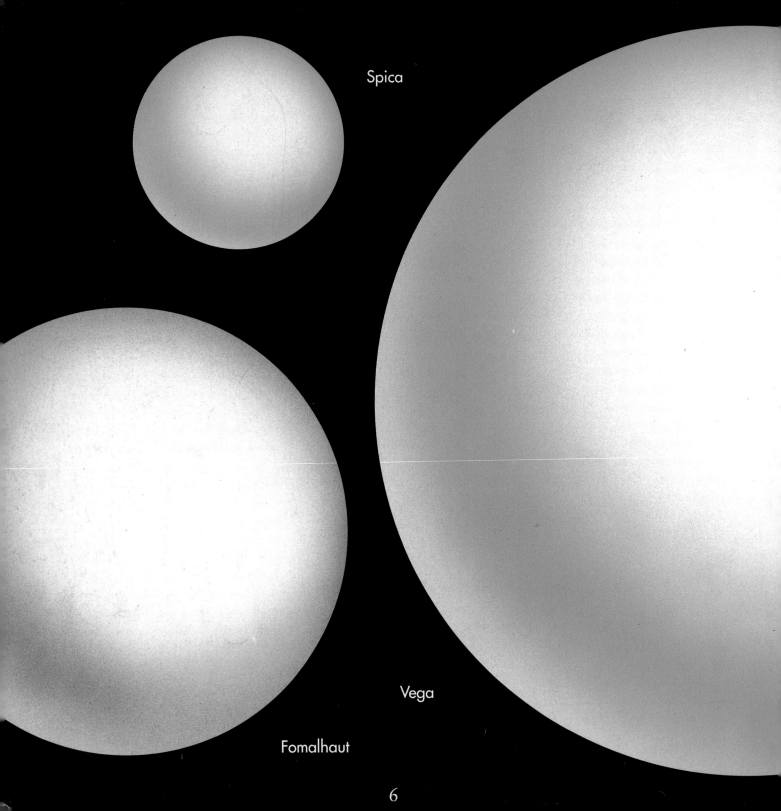

Spica

Vega

Fomalhaut

What the stars are like

The stars look like tiny lamps in the sky, but they are really very big and hot. The sun, which sends us all our light and heat, is only a star.

The Earth moves around the sun, which looks much brighter than any of the other stars because it is much closer to us. The sun is much bigger than the Earth, but we know that some of the stars are much bigger and hotter than the sun. The stars look so small and faint only because they are such a long way away from us.

Our sun

7

How the stars seem to move

If you watch the night sky, you will see all the stars moving very slowly across the sky from east to west. But they are not really moving like this. They seem to do so because the Earth, which is shaped like a ball, is turning around, making one full turn in 24 hours. This makes the sky seem to move, carrying all the stars with it. Also this is why the sun seems to rise in the east and set in the west.

The stars are not fixed in the sky. All of them are moving around, but they are so far away from us that they always appear to be in the same groupings.

The stars we see now look just the same as they did 2,000 years ago. Even their light takes many years to reach us, so we do not see them as they are "now;" we see them as they used to be years ago!

The night sky in this scene of long ago would look no different today.

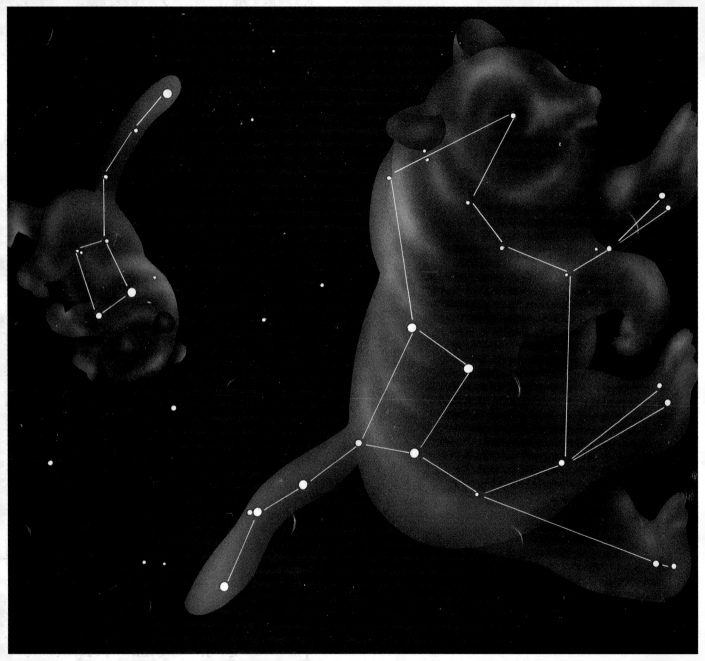

The two bears in the sky

People who lived long ago gave names to the groups of stars, and made up stories about them. One of these stories was about two bears, who were pulled up by their tails and put into the sky. The Great Bear, sometimes called the Big Dipper, is shown by seven stars which make a shape which is very easy to find. The Little Bear is not so bright, but in it we find the north pole of the sky, close to the North Star. Once you have found the North Star you will always be able to find it again, because it does not seem to move at all.

In Australia or New Zealand, the Great Bear is very low in the sky, and you cannot see the Little Bear at all. But you can see new groups, such as the Southern Cross, which are never visible from America.

The Southern Cross

high up when it is winter in America, and summer in Australia. In Orion there are two very bright stars called Betelgeux and Rigel, and three stars in a line which make up the Hunter's Belt.

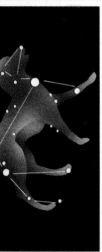

The Great Dog

Not far from Orion is the Great Dog, in which we find the brightest of all the nighttime stars. name is Sirius, but most people just call it the Dog Star. Further south, so that it can never be seen from America, is another very bright star, Canopus. In Australia you can see Canopus in the night sky for most of the year.

The colors of the stars

If you look at the stars, you will see
that they are not all the same

White star (Sirius) color. Our sun is yellow;

most of the nighttime stars look white,

but there are a few which are orange

or red. This is because some of the

stars are hotter than others.

White stars are hotter than yellow

stars, while yellow stars are hotter

than those which are orange or red.

Most of the stars in Orion are white,

but there is one which is red; this is the

one named Betelgeux, but it is often called

Yellow star
(Our sun)

Red star
(Betelgeux)

Orange star
(Aldebaran)

The Horsehead Nebula

How stars are born

Here and there in the night sky we can see patches of dust and gas. There is a special name for them; they are called "nebulae" (pronounced neb-you-lee), from an old word which means "clouds." Inside these clouds, new stars are being born. Long ago, our sun was born in just the same way.

Some of the nebulae are easy to find. There is one in the star group of Orion, the Hunter; you can see it near the three bright stars which make up the

How stars die
The sun, like all the other stars, cannot live forever. When it can no longer shine, it will become very dark and heavy, and then it will become cold and dark. Luckily this will not happen for a very long time, so there is no need to be afraid that the sun will go out. For many millions of years to come the sun will look just the same as it does now.

Some very big stars do not live for so long, and when they can no longer shine they blow up! Sometimes we can see a star doing this. For a few days or weeks it may be very bright, but before long it will fade away.

But remember that the light from the stars takes years to reach us, so that when we watch a star blowing up we are seeing something which really happened a long time ago.

The Milky Way in the night sky

The Milky Way

If you live away from a town, and there are no lights near you, you will be able to see the Milky Way. This looks like a band of light crossing the night sky. It is made up of stars which look as if they are very close together.

This is not really true. The system of stars in which we live is shaped just like two fried eggs put together back to back. When we look along the thick part of the system, we can see many stars, almost one behind the other, and it is this which makes up the Milky Way.

Side view of our galaxy

We have a special name for the system of stars in which we live; we call it the galaxy. In it there are at least a hundred thousand million stars.

Other galaxies

The Milky Way galaxy is not the only one. Like many of the other galaxies, ours is a "spiral." The sun and the Earth lie near the edge of one of the spiral arms.

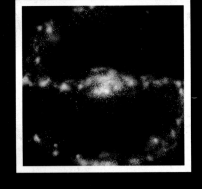

S-shaped galaxy

Most of the galaxies are so far away that their light takes millions of years to reach us. Except for a few of the closer galaxies, all of them are moving away from us, so that the whole universe is spreading out.

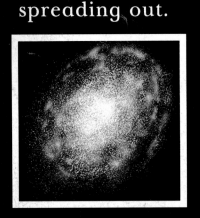

Elliptical galaxy

There are many questions about the universe that we cannot answer yet. We are having an interesting time trying to find these answers and perhaps if you are interested, you will too.

Top view of
our galaxy as it
would be seen from a
spacecraft a million light
years away. The arrow
points to our Earth.

Index